How To Find All Missing Persons / Unsolved Cases. And Collect All Reward Offers. Volume XXX. THE CASE OF JUANITA NIELSEN

DAVID GOMADZA

www.twofuture.world

Copyright © 2024 David Gomadza

All rights reserved.

Paperback **ISBN**: 9798327961258

DEDICATION

To a better future.

CONTENTS

How To Find All Missing Persons /
Unsolved Cases.
And Collect All Reward Offers. Volume XXX
THE CASE OF JUANITA NIELSEN   1

The Afterlife Conversation

and The Council Of Creation.   6

The Killers.   16

ACKNOWLEDGMENTS

Tomorrow's World Order

How To Find All Missing Persons / Unsolved Cases. And Collect All Reward Offers. Volume XXX. THE CASE OF JUANITA NIELSEN

BACKGROUND INFORMATION

The NSW Government, together with the NSW Police Force, has announced a $1 million reward for information as inquiries continue into the 1975 disappearance and suspected murder of Juanita Nielsen.

Homicide Squad Commander, Detective Superintendent Danny Doherty, said detectives will explore every line of inquiry in hope of finally getting justice for Juanita.

Juanita Nielsen – then aged 38 – was last seen at the Carousel Cabaret on Rosyln Street at Kings Cross, on the morning of Friday 4 July 1975 and was later reported missing.

During initial investigations, police uncovered information relating to a conspiracy to kidnap Ms Nielsen on Monday 30 June 1975 – four days prior to her last known sighting.

In late 1977, three men were arrested and charged with conspiracy to kidnap. Two of the men were subsequently convicted, while the third was acquitted.

How To Find All Missing Persons / Unsolved Cases. And Collect All Reward Offers.
Volume XXXIV. THE CASE OF JUANITA NIELSEN

Despite extensive investigations over the years, no one has been charged in relation to Ms Nielsen's disappearance and suspected murder.

Since 1975, NSW Police Force investigators have conducted numerous inquiries in an effort to locate her remains. Despite these efforts, her body has never been found.

In 1982, the NSW Government announced a $50,000 reward for information relating to her disappearance and suspected murder and in 1983, a Coronial Inquest found it was likely Ms Nielsen had died; however, the cause of death was undetermined.

Since that time, the investigation has remained open under Strike Force Euclid, with detectives investigating all information received to identify those involved in Ms Nielsen's disappearance

"We acknowledge that this matter occurred more than four decades ago and that there is very limited opportunity for police to gather further forensic evidence and witness statements," Det Supt Doherty said.

"In turn, it has also become difficult for police to target known persons of interest or associates due to their passing.

"However, it is our hope that someone in the community may have information about Juanita's disappearance, or the location of her remains.

"After nearly half a century of searching for answers, police hope to locate Juanita, so her family may put her to rest," Det Supt Doherty said.

Juanita's cousin, Mr Francis Foy, said his cousin's disappearance has devasted their family for more than four decades.

"Juanita was very much loved by her family and very much missed. Her disappearance and the unknown of what happened to her caused incredible pain for her family," Mr Foy said.

"Our purpose now is to try and find where Juanita's remains are, so that she can be buried respectfully with other members of our family and a memorial can be placed.

"If there is anyone who has information as to what could have happened to Juanita, or where her remains may be, please tell the police. We do hope there is someone or may have associated with people around Kings Cross in 1975 that may be able to shed some light on where her remains are," Mr Foy said.

Anyone with information that may assist Strike Force Euclid detectives is urged to contact Crime Stoppers: 1800 333 000 or https://nsw.crimestoppers.com.au. Information is treated in strict confidence. The public is reminded not to report information via NSW Police social media pages.

TOMORROW'S WORLD ORDER'S PERSPECTIVES

USE OF PREDEFINED AFTERLIFE PARAMETERS

These guide souls the moment it exist the human body on its journey to Yahweh the creator these define what to do and what to expect as you go to hell or heaven if a souk leaves earth it enters ozone orbit and instantly everything reboots for it to start a new phase of life after living the earth's body now what happens is that it enters the ozone orbit and a simply click caused by the sudden drop of pressure from -1186 to – 20 means the bottom shaft of the soul will lift rapidly and this pushes its back into the air higher than its head best example is a penguin but with real human legs and head just the shape now God created a life predefined program for them instead of asking what should I do and where should I go they instantly know from predefined stencils if you did well and talked most about God then heaven is for you if you did evil and talked more about the devil then the devil is yours now if we Ask what can be of humans without souks this is the answer dead forever your soul is you a new transformation to the electromagnetic waves life where you see Yahweh for the first time and praise him and wish you had seen him a long time ago because of his Majesty and will always be there forever now what are all these you may ask these are rules to be guided by in the creation court in short it has everything humans know about the judges and the presiding judge who will always be Yahweh and 84 angels surrounding the altar 28 high priests who always say Yahweh have mercy on humans and 74 smaller courts priests who always say Yahweh has mercy on humans and 96 princesses who say glory to Yahweh forever and ever amen we have 96 elders who always say if I can why he can't meaning if the devil can drink blood why can't Yahweh who created the devil and blood do the same now this is not the same as saying if the devil can kill why can Yahweh its more on professional grounds rather than challenging now if we look at the inside of the court we have 81 priests surrounding the altar who say Yahweh be merciful to humans but if they disobey you we put hem on trial for you and kill them for you almighty Yahweh inside this is a round circle where Yahweh sits

and asks questions now if we look deep inside the court you will see that there are other things that resemble earth high courts like benches and chairs 10 times human sizes for the gods who are so enormous 2 are equal to 84 billion humans in size
predefined parameters for humans after death as in know what is inside is a large size of books the book of creation is among them with 10897867892836789012348678901245861789011 pages and is divided into humans first then chapter for animals then a chapter for angles then a chapter for gods and a chapter for Joseph Yahweh's best friend and a chapter for Yahweh's best friend's wife Anna and a chapter for Yahweh's wife Catitighit and lastly a chapter for Yahweh and recently a chapter for davidgomadza as Yahweh's representative on earth marking the new beginnings starting in 2025

1. tell us who killed you
2. tell us what killed you
3. tell us why and who killed you
4. tell us why you died
5. tell us what could have been done and is not done
6. tell us what could be and why
7. tell is when this happened
8. tell us why this is so
9. tell us why this is so
10. what can be done to improve this

What does the book of creation say about davidgomadza David Gomadza is the first and last ruler to be appointed by Yahweh fir the next 25 billion years and will act as his representative on earth deciding cases and upholding his principles on earth and as such has been entitled to 489 trillion dollars in assets this number signifies eternity among humans and the beginning of a new Era chapter 7867892802893862841890287689018320867890123486789018236487289128610 Creation manual the new Era of new electromagnetic wave conduit signed and dated by Yahweh himself on 27may2024 at 237800 Yatime creation.universe.ya.start.end.find.davidgomadza.ya.askya.ya

Ask.read.creation.manucreation.universe.ya.start.end.find.davidgoma askya.ya

Ask.rulesofthecourt.start.now.start
David Gomadza welcome the rules of court are guiding principles that tell you what to do and how to do it first you must always say I believe in the court of creation and I shall abide by he rules of this court and shall always do things according to the rules of this court in deciding the cases I am assigned to you must ask what can be done so that you know all your options before making choices the court system will make it easy to check files and ask the outcomes of the decision ask the court the final decision in any case.

THE AFTERLIFE CONVERSATION AND THE COUNCIL OF CREATION'S ANAYLSIS.

juanita nielsen electromagnetic wave 08983678902848367890284109285678902345678901836780098 who was 38 and killed by rstop sevt who said what does it take to convince someone that i love her then toss her out that very day and now act according to what she do
1. if she still want me then tell me the same and chuck me out as well the next day
2. must ask what can be done to improve things but walk away because i must threaten to do the same
3. i must insist that she leaves safety bit if she returns then wait for her and kill her and bury her in the same grave as someone as her first name only
4. if she ask why then tell her that this is wrong you loving me after few days
5. tell her to go in peace if she refused escort her but don't kill her now at this time he is staying with his mum and wants her to move out but they don't want her to know so how does he tell his own mum she is not wanted then he asked what can be said about mothers who can't leave the property for their sons but for their lovers and his aty said that hurts but there are a lot of things you can do like make it a

crime scene for 10 years go and do time you are not wanted anywhere get a hooked and harass her here and go to jail and come back your mother's lover won't take the house and he said okay but what about without doing time then it said then you need to ask god all humans will give you a crime that does not involve any intelligence simply because we are humans but must be done but if you ask me what can be done then take a beautiful woman and marry her then let other have sex with her and divorce her but say the house is out of boundary then sell the house give a cut to your mum for bringing you up that's it the lover actually give him your and say i marry my own mum for the house he laughed and said if you can think like this then why do we need a god for everyone is saying have you seen god lately but there is no god but then with such thinking then you can be a god without the capital g and and hug me and said we were created to look for god and copy him in everyday so that we can create

juanita nielsen was killed by a one asert atorsp who said can if you can then said if you can can i then opened the door for her then said what can be said about us marrying today she said i love to i was thinking about marriage too then they started staying together then on the third day he said i love you then she said but is included me too then he said it's too early for you so you are not serious then take your things and go and she refused she said we belong together now after marriage there is no separation then she said okay but i will come back then he said then something might happen she said okay but you said let's get married so we must get married then talk later he agreed then they got married that night and he said okay what will you do if i kick you out of the house and she said why what will i have done he said in the future house is still my mum when she die then she said oh then i don't know i thought you are talking about now he said no i mean the future and she smiled and said i never been refused before so it's strange for me to hear these things then he said i want to ask you a question when did they ask you what to do then she said who then he said the police and he looked surprised that she just looked at him and he smiled and said they want to take the house but because my ma wants to give it to her man in case she dies now he said if we can then can we but so what can be of woman who want to be married but can't play the game and end up dead then she said i don't want to die if it does not work out i can leave even now i thought you really wanted to get married you just want the name without the marriage right is that so but it does not work that way do you know it works both ways love me to love me kick me to go simple okay let's fuck because if we don't then the marriage is broken so he fucked her the best listening to her and she squirt first then said i cum can i sleep because when i cum i have to sleep for an hour then he agreed only on condition that she say i love you she said i love you and slept then he waited 20 minutes then 40 then 60 then 80 then 100 minutes then said i want to sleep too but how can i without fuck and she said you should have wanked when i was asleep but on top of me as we are married if you wait then you will wait forever because i sleep sometimes for hours after u cum the reason why no one wants to marry me then he looked cheated and said we just got married we can annual then what's the point if i have to look elsewhere for sex let's just say it's okay for now but you must change too for this to work okay i love you and tired of looking for sex somewhere else why you don't sacrifice for me i gave you somewhere to live forever and she said but you said only when your mother died then let's start then then he said no don't make the mistake of trying to push my mum in the grave you will need a friend to talk to that's your best friend if you want this to work eventually she will die but don't push her to the ground i would rather lose you because she dies i die too this is how close i am with her okay but shouldn't you be happy you can bring your mother too and these 2 spend time talking while you watch porn or something she laughed and said maybe bring another man who wants sex you rush everything so fast i am always hungry and he looked lost ah i get it its boring with me because i am too fast in everything she said yes but to the boring part and he said but we are married shouldn't we be talking about this over dinner she said who will cook and he said i can cook i cook for my mum why not cook for my wife if she is too tired but she cried and said i can't cook that's why i am crying i never cooked my mum said marry a rich man and where do i find this rich man you we fight on first day of sex i don't think so maybe let's annual now while there is time i go to someone else who want me for

How To Find All Missing Persons / Unsolved Cases. And Collect All Reward Offers.
Volume XXXIV. THE CASE OF JUANITA NIELSEN

sex not to please his mother so she cried and said if you want then let's split up i go while nothing happened so that i don't worry whether i am pregnant or not so she quickly got her stuff and started packing and he realized that she meant and remembered that he had portrayed shelf as rich and looked so extra ordinary than this poor mummy's boy so she rushed to the toilet and took her stuff and said i go bye and left before he realised the real reason while she cried then they would not be a way out so she said i got and slammed door so that your mum know i left then quickly got into the car and left but he realised that she might have stole the house documents on first day and wrote her name then agreed to get married but all this in good will then realised that he is scared to touch the papers because of his mother and said i want you to know we are married now so house is in my name and she flipped and said go out today because this is forgery and you can be sent to prison so she run away but he stopped the car by shouting you left something continuously before he stopped and said what can we do about this she said now nothing i wrote my name on the house's papers its not possible anymore without losing face driver go don't stop and he said where are the papers and she said where i left then then he said let's go together and show me i think it's fair to ask than to say i left them there then not find out let's go the driver wait for you outside ask him first she said no let's go i am the one paying you not him so let's go my life is in danger and you bet a Crooke it's not even his mums house its in a male name house so no go drive the driver started driving and he said that's my other name not the one she knows so you can't take my wife if i say so okay driver and he said ok i call the police first to separate you because she does not like you no woman run away from a good husband okay so wait one minute and he called the police and they said okay wait there too a few minutes but he opened the door and grabbed her hand and pulled her so hard her arm dislodged from the socket but she did not yell but just said ouch my arm look if i can go back he will kill me he told this person so and he looked lost and the driver said let her go away first then you arrange to meet and then talk he agreed then she jumped back in and he strike the driver with a hammer so hard that he did not say anything and jumped into the car and opened the bonnet and quickly drove off locking the doors

How To Find All Missing Persons / Unsolved Cases. And Collect All Reward Offers.
Volume XXXIV. THE CASE OF JUANITA NIELSEN

heading to the highway then stopped in the middle of the road and said let's go to our home our new home we can start again she did not understand what was going on then he said what can we do with this mess and she said don't kill me and he sighed no we are married i don't want you kill you i want to start a family with you not death so he said for once listen to me i am not going to kill you but to trust you and only you

we have seen what is not love with this case when people meet and start staying together that can result in death because these two just met and started staying together doing everything lovers do with put knowing each other that much resulting in death as simple as that now what has been said is that these two would have made it better if they had taken time to get to know each that means 2 people in a relationship must love each other enough to trust each other and work together in this case the man thought she stole house documents otherwise she was planning to come the next day and perform hard for him she realised that she needed excuse so she pretended she had signed papers so that he say okay go then tomorrow say can i come back since he had checked that the papers were not forged meaning a good start for all the court of creation has little doubt that this would have made him soften but was a good start then she said i had to go before sex and before he penetrated this for a man is a no no because a man has gene 24 that says penetrate first then negotiate meaning that without penetration the tamper is always high if we look at this case then we can say that there has been some mishaps happening along the way he killed the driver with a hammer meaning no way out if it was a joke then this would have sealed her fate but she handled it clearly by not even bothering about the driver and said the most idiot ever and she looked at him and said how many times i told him to drive off idiot the most stupid i have ever seen and scream instantly as rstop grabbed her neck while driving and said i am smart enough to know when you want to die all i did was to love you so what happened is that he wanted to push her out of the car while driving so that he will say she jumped out of the car and said

i can if you can but then he stopped and said don't drive a man nuts why you can't give me sex when i want it answer so i know your real

How To Find All Missing Persons / Unsolved Cases. And Collect All Reward Offers.
Volume XXXIV. THE CASE OF JUANITA NIELSEN

reasons she said i was tired and needed good rest and he said you still want we go back or we separate everything don't matter now i killed the taxi driver but we can cover up it so that we are together forever that is if you like she said okay and they drove back home but on return the body was not there and he didn't show fear and parked the taxi driver car home and went in and took a shower but when he came out the car had gone and she returned breathing hard and took a shower too and they slept and had great sex in the morning that she said pregnant me so that he can't feel used or cheated so he did actually counting and timing his ejaculated and her dropping of the egg until a click sparked him that said fertilization achieved so loud he threw up out of panic and she said my aty i got it when i was a lonely kid to play with he laughed and said i have one but mine never talks they laughed and talked together then he said what can 2 adults do after great sex i think today you best even the gods on sex for sure she had spread her legs like never before with her aty teaching her how to give sex forever to break records that for the first time he cried and said if sex is that good with you why do we fight that much and she said that was only once because i didn't want to lose you thinking i am a pro but my aty teaches me what you like during sex but does yours teach you what i want or i have to tell it and he looked shocked he realised why she had not slept he said it just said let her sleep then she smiled and instantly slept deep sleep without a word but only because she started to hear his thoughts before he say things that he asked him if he whisper to her aty but he said no then realised that someone now was listening to them and said what if someone listens to us do we have anything to be afraid of and he said nothing i give no shit to shit and she smiled and slept and when she woke up she was in heaven asking for her husband who make her squirt and screamed very hard to find out that she had no vagina and was not dreaming as she looked an 8th of her size and said who did this and why when i am st my peak devil shit come out i kill you i swear i hate you i was cheated and robbed i just slept and here i am i refuse to speak to all you devil shits i give no shit to shits send me back right now Yahweh felt like crying old age removes all my powers only my representative can and does have powers to do all this which is rebirth now but in your case probably rebirth then rebirth in that

How To Find All Missing Persons / Unsolved Cases. And Collect All Reward Offers.
Volume XXXIV. THE CASE OF JUANITA NIELSEN

first its the baby rebirth then the mother rebirth but all at the same code 878678902878902348671237892841023689828 4 would work through one instance but now we can't we have to wait for Yahweh's representative to come and do this otherwise it is impossible she then said but you are god but why so many heads but she said okay then send my right now if you wait too long then it won't be possible because my body will die they all looked at her and said where will you stay then she said with mu husband the one who loves me and she said rstop and smiled then god then sent her a vision of what happened see for yourself who killed you and how then she saw rstop saying tomorrow god will understand why because i tried everything and all she wants is to sleep therefore i cancel the marriage today at the office i said she run away and he agreed and cancelled the register he had wrote us in then she looked lost as he brought his mother and started having sex together and said i know it hurts but then look how he killed you and replayed the vision where he sat on her nose and drunk a bottle of vodka like liquid without her making and noise with her spirit escaping only after everything stopped making sure it looks at who sat on them and nearly dying to see that it was his mother who sat on her noise without any clothes with her vagina on top of her nose that makes sense to her now why she did not fight this is because the vagina produces mild carbon dioxide that means the person cannot choke bur can easily faint first then lose consciousness then say i need food because all this is covered by the need for food that much that she wakes up but in heaven because the food she needs is that of Yahweh in silkpasty if you give her normal food she wake up in hell therefore his mother realised that silent death was the best he could not enter when his step dad his look alike is having sex with her he has to wait but his girlfriend is there too so now in human terms they shaped for sex the first night and knowing no woman have sex the first night but the second night meaning she want him for marriage customary in european language now this is the court of creation verdict she was carbon monoxide poisoned by her mother-in-law vagina while in deep sleep after having great sex cummings 5 rounds a record for her after her own aty stayed awake all night making things worse on promise of taking her body when she dies only of gasses instead of the dreaded cancers therefore the

How To Find All Missing Persons / Unsolved Cases. And Collect All Reward Offers.
Volume XXXIV. THE CASE OF JUANITA NIELSEN

court of creation said that atert stert caused her death by sitting on her literally but could mean used real carbon monoxide gas but her internals speaks only of suffocation that simulate strangulation but more likely as above her readings are
anus 20
breathe 8
atom suspense 2 max 87 average 54
oxygen 2 minimum 70 maximum 120
carbon dioxide 80 minimum 2 average 6
abdominal fluids 10 average 2 meaning poison response
water 80 average 20 max 60 another indicator of poisoning
breathing hard min soft average 8
avl 80 minimum 20 average 70
atm 20 average 20 maximum 80 meaning some form of poisoning that needs more fluids like substances used to remove poisons
ast this is to refuse if you don't want her level was 4 it should be 200 meaning tampering and if we ask this means that someone was tampering with some of her unless this is her problem that make other man refuse to marry her if we look closer it becomes clear now that sleep was her greatest disadvantage and as such had every reason to avoid everything that caused deep sleep
the end
atert stert god my name is atert sevt i am the mother of aropt sevt my son who killed a taxi driver of rtop taxis and wirelessly phoned me to clean his body and send it to the mortuary as i worked there when i woke up the other day his wife slept on the couch as he drink vodka like liquid then said where are your chemicals you use on dead people my wife is not moving then he said i can't seem to understand what happened she said after that tea she slept like a baby and never woke up i make the greatest tea ever and as such believe that it tasted too good enough to take her to heaven straight away she smiled and said still the house is still mine and i can do what i want with it then she said do you want tea she had left and he said okay and took it and drunk all of it that she said no not you what are you doing and instantly called the hospital and she said i had food poisoning come quickly then it came and took her instead but she did not die it happen to be that he shaped just tge moment she looked

How To Find All Missing Persons / Unsolved Cases. And Collect All Reward Offers. Volume XXXIV. THE CASE OF JUANITA NIELSEN

away but because the chemicals she used
1. actyole acts fast in hot liquids like tea
2. actole she used acts well in hot liquids
3. atel works fast in hot liquid
4. aclert she used works well in hot liquid all these four chemicals were bended together in the ration of 20% actyole 25 % active 30% atel and lastly 25% aclert a dangerous cocktail but all this used in cleaning dead bodies at the private mortuary she worked at wherein turns out is a family run business cleansing dead people hence their expertise with dead that her daughter in law did not see it coming days after artop said if she can then i can but then dialed the police and said my wife died she just woke up dead then sergent atop said you must be joking who wakes up dead you better tell us the truth or else we still take the house even after the crime scene had ended he laughed and said look at these shits they still can do their jobs they fixated with stealing our house that they refuse to believe the truth then you give us your version of events see if it fits the template created by this one they said your mother sat on her with her vagina on her nose so that she can't breathe and rubbed it on face smoothing her to death if this is the police this is how they see this case and he laughed and said i laugh at these idiots they tend not to see the truth because they want the house which is not theirs isn't it stealing

my name is artop sevt people call me asert though but i like my mother so much one day i said i want to marry you and she laughed and said you are going to get your father killed and i said by who and he said by the police and i laughed so hard a farted and nearly shifted myself and never talked about it until my father died and ever since i blamed myself until today i gave her a chance to revenge and see killed her using all cleaning chemicals from aftop a mortuary service without a trace or anyone knowing how she said the police will say i put my vagina on her but 4 strong highly toxic but untraceable chemicals chemicals sent her to Yahweh without a trace and she said you took mine and i said no it was pc atop who shot him in the head and said an intruder at 85 grandle road over while i look through the window she said it's okay it's not your fault he used to threaten them because he said kill yourself get yourself a gun o0ne day i shot you if

How To Find All Missing Persons / Unsolved Cases. And Collect All Reward Offers. Volume XXXIV. THE CASE OF JUANITA NIELSEN

you keep asking what value is my house
atert sevt she said grandma if we are to stay together then you can move in with us if the name on the house changed touching her tummy i knew that feeling that i had to kill her because i was going to be homeless so i cooked 20% actole 30% aclote and 25% azole 25% aloet then made her tea she smiled beautifully and i said sweet dreams and she said you too grandma i think you know why from babies to grandma we are 2 but 3 then she said when i wake up i will tell you why you will be the richest grandma in her brain i am an only child too and i have a house in jaunita asert the reason i came here was to find out if artop asert is related to my father when i checked all the house papers i knew they were fake asert because their real surname is sevrt not asert that's why i refused sex the first night i just need to change back my name to asert from nielsen that was imposed on me by the police especially pc atop who said if i can but then what and cooked his gun once and went in then said what can be done and came out pc atop i am the best sharp shooter i only joined the force because i found out that i can easily kill so far i killed atorp senior at his own house for his house if i want to be honest but it's a job because nothing has ever gave us strength than capital gains tax it means gaining the capital for a house the boss explained you want it you work for it if you don't someone else take its that simple and hide evidence until 20 years then get 12% in cash to say thank you or $1million dollars which ever is greater usually since these capital gains taxes started not even a single case or reward was solved by the public but all by the cop involved in the killing.
juanita nielsen not found but juanita asert found god i died without knowing i think someone poisoned me i smells dead chemicals as my aty keep saying it calculates 25 % acerol 25 % aterol ?30% anopert and 20 % azetc but keep saying why mortuary games in body tell source to me then dies as well but i think my mother in law but i love her so much i said i can marry you if you want drop your son and she said fir me or the house and i said i am joking but i never loved anyone like her before very generous and outgoing but very secretive about her work until today she work with dead people i have games that smell like choke or burnt oil inside me and i have a baby i have a

baby coming soon and i want you to know that i will look after her but the foams may have been meant for the baby oh i died again today and she died again and god could have worked her up and if he had his powers but then he didn't.
the end
juanita nielsen [asert] itsis possible but i lost all the powers over years but i can get back the power if his representative can say a code that make it possible as rebirth rebirth

THE KILLER, THE CONFESSIONS AND THE COORDINATES

juanita nielsen not found but juanita asert found god i died without knowing i think someone poisoned me i smells dead chemicals as my aty keep saying it calculates 25 % acerol 25 % aterol ?30% anopert and 20 % azetc but keep saying why mortuary games in body tell source to me then dies as well but i think my mother in law but i love her so much i said i can marry you if you want drop your son and she said fir me or the house and i said i am joking but i never loved anyone like her before very generous and outgoing but very secretive about her work until today she work with dead people i have games that smell like choke
atert sevt she said grandma if we are to stay together then you can move in with us if the name on the house changed touching her tummy i knew that feeling that i had to kill her because i was going to be homeless so i cooked 20% actole 30% aclote and 25% azole 25% aloet then made her tea she smiled beautifully and i said sweet dreams and she said you too grandma i think you know why from babies to grandma we are 2 but 3

…I found God…visit www.twofuture.world

THE CLAIM

the reward offer

THE COLLECTION

www.twofuture.world/donate

ABOUT DAVID GOMADZA

visit www.twofuture.world

signed david gomadza
ask.davidgomadzaauthorised.licensed.checkya.askya.ya

09 June 2024 00.36 pm
scotland
00447719210295
davidgomadza@hotmail.com
info@twofuture.world

www.ingramcontent.com/pod-product-compliance
Lightning Source LLC
Chambersburg PA
CBHW032312240526
45464CB00023BA/2997